HOW to DIE

ALONE

The Foolproof Guide to ^Not Helping Yourself

MO WELCH

Workman Publishing • New York

Library of Congress Cataloging-in-Publication Data is available.

ISBN: 978-1-5235-0426-8

Design by Jean-Marc Troadec and Terri Ruffino

Workman books are available at special discounts when purchased in bulk for premiums and sales promotions as well as for fund-raising or educational use. Special editions or book excerpts can also be created to specification. For details, contact the Special Sales Director at the address below, or send an email to specialmarkets@workman.com.

Workman Publishing Co., Inc.
225 Varick Street
New York, NY 10014-4381
workman.com

WORKMAN is a registered trademark of Workman Publishing Co., Inc.

Printed in China

First printing March 2019

10 9 8 7 6 5 4 3 2 1

For all the Blairs
out there.

And Sam.

CONTENTS

INTRODUCTION: MEET BLAIR

Hi. I'm Blair. I'm the friend you never had, probably because your parents called me "a little depressing" and "too cynical" and "Where's her dad?" I may have a dark perspective on life, but I'm always honest—and in a world littered with gratingly positive YouTube personalities, honesty has got to be worth something, right?

This world has enough self-help books. They offer steps for overcoming social anxiety and prescribe no-meat, no-carb, no-fun diets to help you lose weight and your will to live. Those books work for some people. Not me. I don't want to waste my life reading about how to improve my life. I want to waste my life having one-sided conversations with my cat.

So here is the self-help guide for *not* helping yourself. This guide is for the brave souls who want to live their lives at home in sweatpants, eating pizza, bagels, and/or pizza bagels for every meal.

In this book, I will show you how to become an antisocial hermit, how to fail at your boring job, how to sabotage your friendships, and much more! I'll even offer tombstone suggestions to help you celebrate successfully dying alone. You can thank me later, when we're all dead.

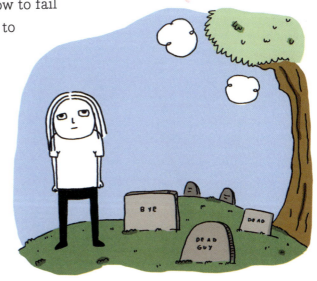

BECOME AN ANTI SOCIAL HERMIT

At a certain point, attending parties becomes more of a chore than a reward. Maybe it's because there's no element of surprise. Every party is identical to the one that came before it. You fat-shame yourself as you pick out an outfit, you get to the party too early, you talk to people you'll never see again, and you spend the whole night imagining yourself at home watching murder documentaries in your sweatpants.

So why bother with parties? Or people? Or anything? If you truly want to die alone, start by being alone *now*. Never leave your house or see any friends or family again! Except for maybe your cat.

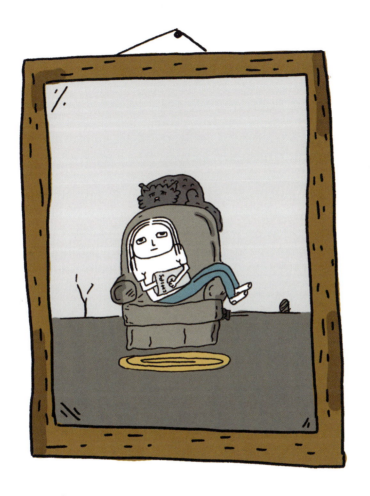

Portrait of a woman flaking
on all her plans.

Hermit Tip #1

If you're uncertain about going out,
just say no.

SHOULD I GO OUT TONIGHT?
YES!
I THINK IT'S BROKEN.

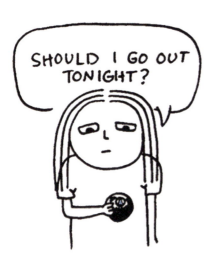

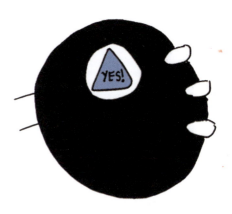

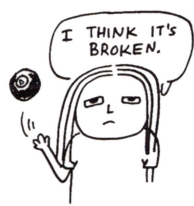

HOW TO HIDE WHEN YOU SEE SOMEONE YOU KNOW IN PUBLIC

1 Jump into the middle of that clothing rack.

2 Lie down in that bush.

3 Blend into that tree.

4 Walk behind that server. (Keep the same pace.)

5 Hold that baby. Look, you're just a passing mom now.

6 Give back that baby. You're not ready for that kind of responsibility.

7 Jump into that sewer. The Teenage Mutant Ninja Turtles were regular turtles before they saw Gerard, the friend they didn't want to talk to.

We play hide-and-seek as kids to prepare us for seeing someone we know in public as adults.

7

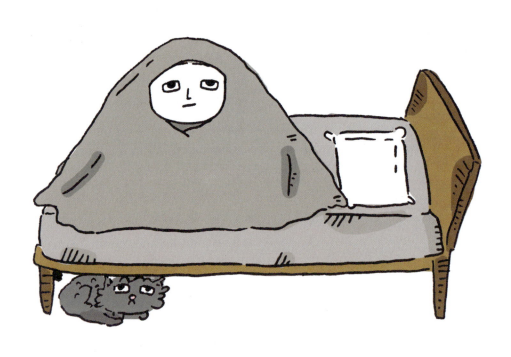

Keep Calm and Stay at Home.

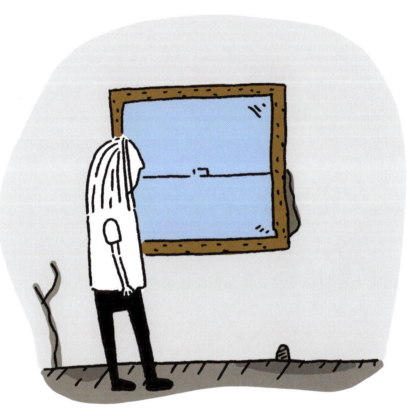

Today's forecast:
Lots of people. Better stay in.

Hermit Tip #2

You don't need to have a life if you follow people online who have lives.

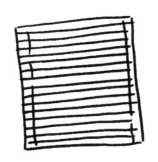

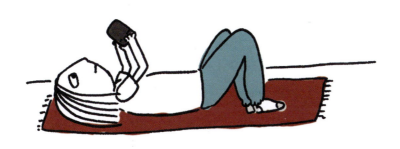

I think I'll go for a scroll inside.

EXCUSES TO USE WHEN FLAKING ON YOUR BORING FRIENDS

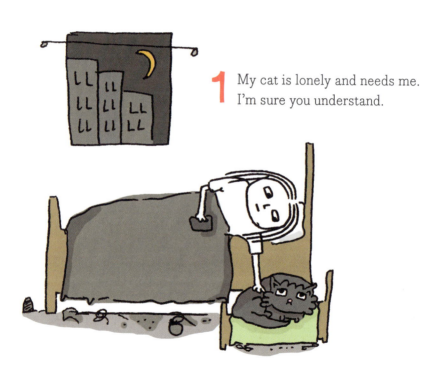

1 My cat is lonely and needs me. I'm sure you understand.

2 Umm, exercise? Yeah, exercise. I need to go to the gym.

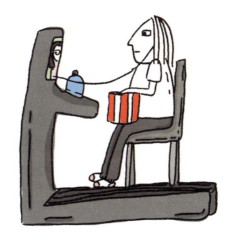

3 I gotta organize my cereal boxes by sunset.

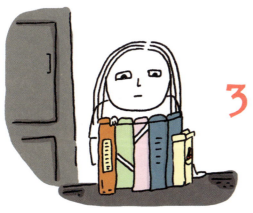

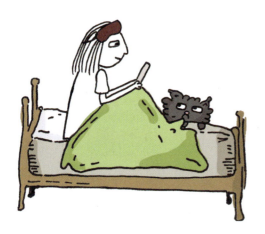

4 I have to work late. (You don't need to mention that what you're working on is stalking ex-friends on social media, and your office is a bed. And your coworker is a cat.)

5 I'm busy watching every murder documentary available.

6 I need to pray. (Trust me, nobody will fight you on this one.)

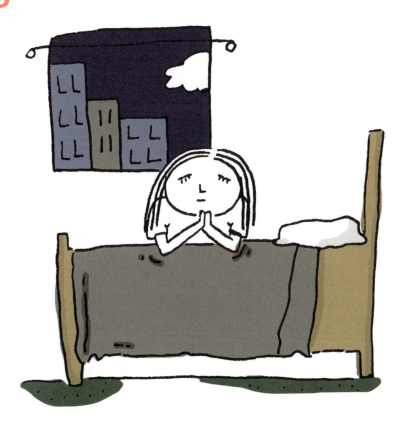

5 ONE-WAY CONVERSATIONS TO HAVE WITH YOUR CAT

1 What have you been doing all day?

2 Where do we go when we die?

3 Can you believe [SPOILER] happened in *Game of Thrones*?

4 Do you think Stacey and Tim will make it?

5 Be honest—will you eat me when I die?

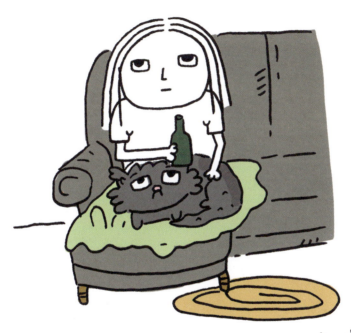

Pets are the reason I don't technically drink alone.

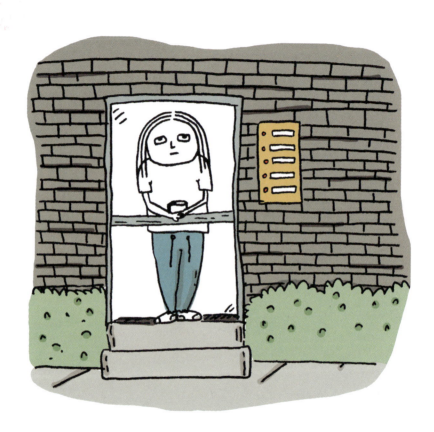

Almost leaving is basically leaving.

I think I'm in love.

6 WAYS TO SPRUCE UP YOUR SWEATPANTS WHEN YOU LEAVE YOUR HOUSE FOR 5 MINUTES

1 Add a belt.

2 Sequins!

3 Wear a pair as a scarf.

4 Hook them to your butt—look, you have tux tails!

5 Turn the pockets inside out. By the time people ask, "Is that a new trend?" your five minutes outside will be up.

6 Clean them! (Just kidding. Don't.)

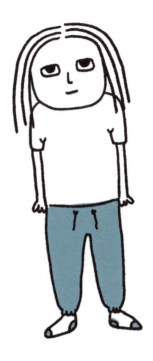

Sweatpants Party of One.

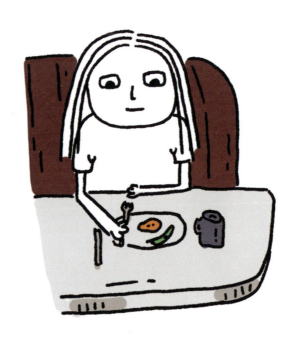

Eating alone is the new
eating with people.

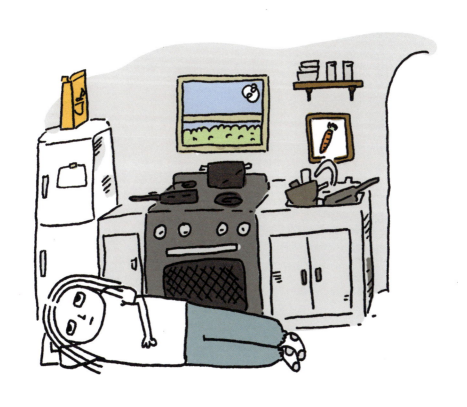

Completing chores is such a chore.

Hermit Tip #3

Stare out the window with a blank expression on your face until your neighbors finally label you "that weird cat lady." Well deserved.

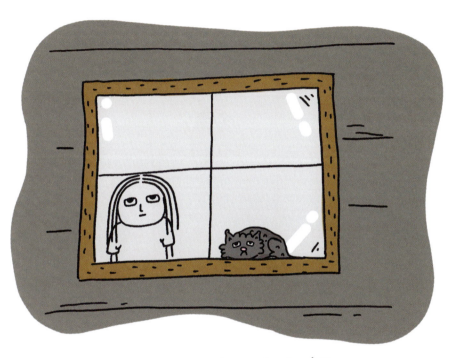

I pay a lot of rent to be
this miserable inside.

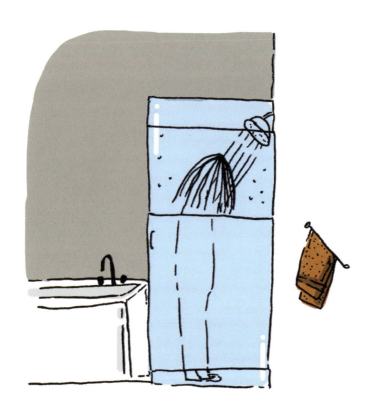

when you live alone, showering
is always on your to-do list.

Oh, the Places You Won't Go!

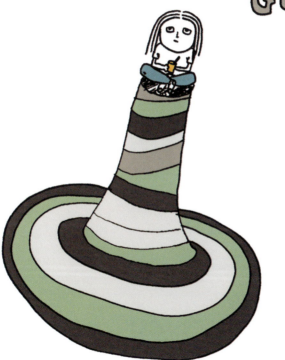

Hermit Tip #4

Feel free to plan events. Just don't invite anyone to them.

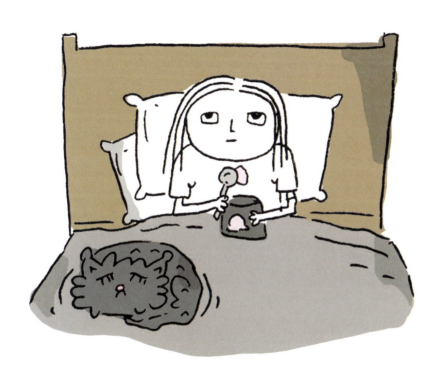

Look. An Ice Cream Anti-Social.

ARE YOU A TRUE HERMIT?

This checklist will help you determine if you have mastered the art of hermiting.

- [ ] YOUR PREFERRED EVENING ACTIVITY IS BINGE-WATCHING TV SHOWS.

- [ ] THE NUMBER OF BLANKETS ON YOUR COUCH SURPASSES THE NUMBER OF DECORATIVE PILLOWS.

- [ ] YOU LOSE YOUR REMOTE CONTROL AT LEAST ONCE A NIGHT.

- [ ] WHEN YOU GET HOME AFTER WORK THERE'S A FAT CHANCE YOU'LL LEAVE.

- [ ] YOU PANIC WHEN A FRIEND ASKS YOU OUT FOR DRINKS.

- [ ] YOUR ONLY REGULAR VISITOR IS THE FOOD DELIVERY PERSON.

- [ ] OH, AND THAT DELIVERY PERSON IS ON SPEED DIAL.

- [ ] WHEN IT RAINS YOU FEEL ALIVE.

- [ ] YOU TALK TO YOUR CAT IN COMPLETE SENTENCES.

- [ ] YOU STAY IN AND FILL OUT CHECKLISTS IN A BOOK CALLED *HOW TO DIE ALONE*.

Did you check seven or more boxes? Congrats. You're a certified hermit. But you're not the only one. This world is filled with us! (We may never know the real number, though, because hermits refuse to go outside to fill out a survey.)

EARN THE WORST FRIEND AWARD

Friends are overrated. You only really need them when you're in school so you don't have to sit alone in the cafeteria, like Steve. (Poor Steve.) That sneaking suspicion that you should "lose touch" with your friends after graduation? Trust it!

Friends never tell you the truth anyway. They want you to like them, so they just say what you want to hear. Like, "You should *totally* get bangs" or "You should *totally* text your ex" or "You *totally* don't have spinach in your teeth, Blair. Say cheese!"

If you're really serious about dying alone, you'll have to make your friends go away sooner or later. Not sure how? Just follow my tips, and you too can earn the prestigious Worst Friend Award!

1ST
WORST
FRIEND
AWARD

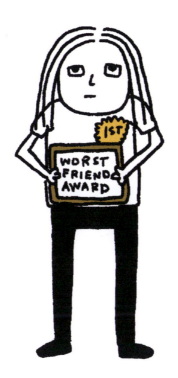

Worst Friend Tip #1

If you get bored while talking to a
childhood friend, just bring up an old
resentment from high school. You'll
fight for hours!

You still owe me #3 for that double cheeseburger 10 years ago...

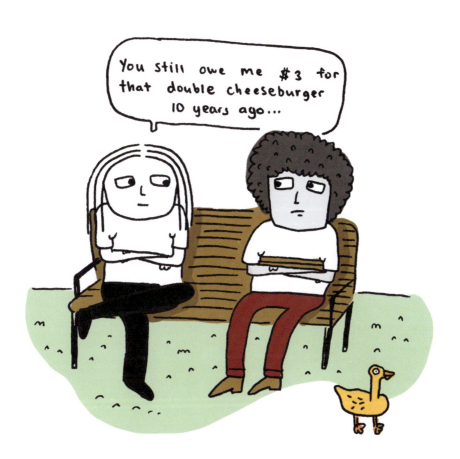

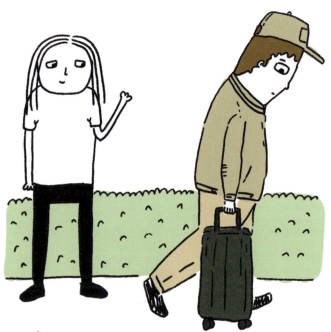

I'm comfortable with any level of friendship before the "taking you to the airport" level.

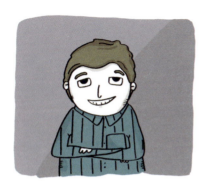

NOW, WHAT DOES YOUR TATTOO
MEAN, EXACTLY?

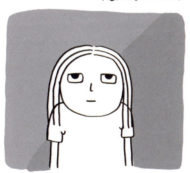

IT MEANS "I HATE SMALL
TALK WITH STRANGERS."

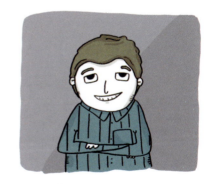

INTERESTING. SO, WHERE
YA FROM?

Worst Friend Tip #2

If you're out of food and money,
raid your rich friend's fridge. If they
catch you, say you "miss hanging
with them."

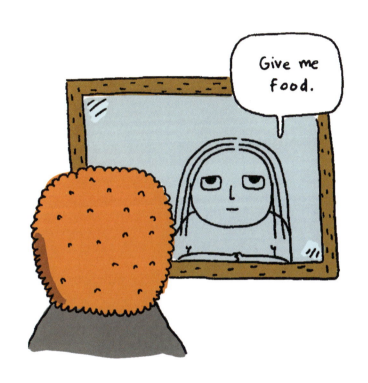

I treat my friends' houses like
24-hour drive-thrus.

TRUTHS YOUR FRIENDS DON'T WANT TO HEAR BUT YOU WILL SAY ANYWAY

1 Maybe your mom's right (this works for anything).

2 Yeah, you definitely picked the wrong career.

3 You are the last person I'd call if I were arrested.

4 I take short naps when you tell stories about your life.

5 Yes, you've told me that "funny" story already. Seventeen times, actually.

6 You can't see the patterns that are killing your dating life (but I can).

7 Your relationship with your pet is disturbing.

8 Yes, your haircut does look like it was paid for with a coupon.

9 Your new boyfriend is exactly the same as your old boyfriend.

10 You have bad breath.

My mom said I shouldn't have married Tim.
Uh-she's right.

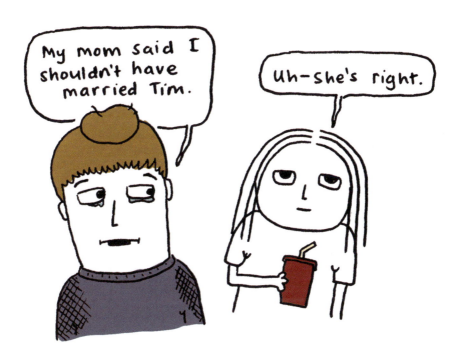

Worst Friend Tip #3

If you *have* to go to brunch, DO
NOT sit in the middle of the booth.
People will talk past you and it will
be annoying. Grab an end seat so
you can run away to the bathroom
whenever you want.

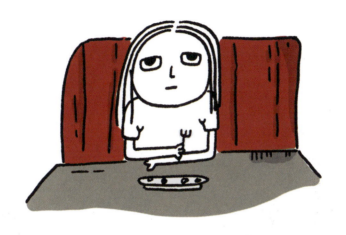

I'd rather eat my own arm than go to brunch with you and your college friends.

REASONS WHY I DON'T WANT TO GO TO YOUR WEDDING

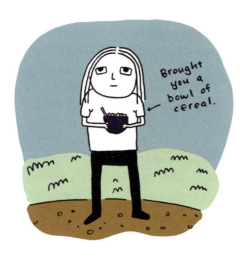

Brought you a bowl of cereal.

1 I can't afford any of the gifts on your registry.

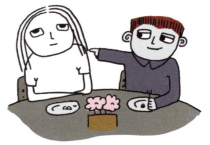

2 I know you'll punish the single people by seating them at the kids' table.

3 I don't respect your relationship after seeing you at your bachelorette party.

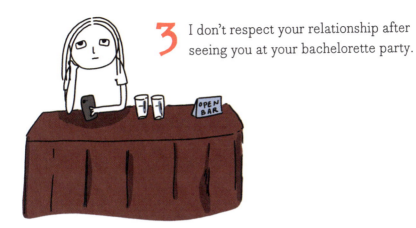

4 I hate that part when I'm forced to catch flowers with the other singles.

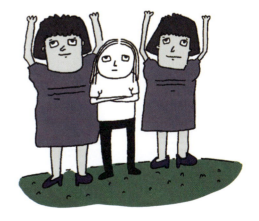

5 Vows bore me.

6 Most of all, I'd rather be here.

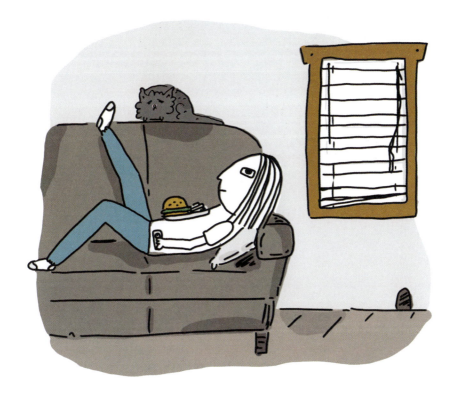

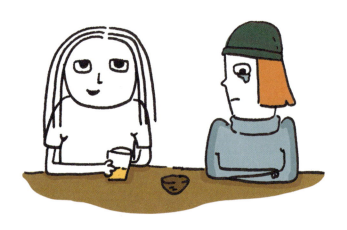

I'm not laughing at your heartbreak.
I'm laughing because emotions make
me uncomfortable.

When you're pretending to be
like your adult friends:

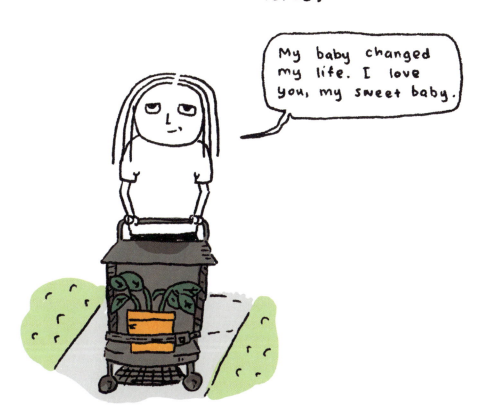

Worst Friend Tip #4

Give your cat a human name so
when you say you can't go out
because you already have plans with
Joan, your friends assume you've
met someone cooler than them.

JOAN

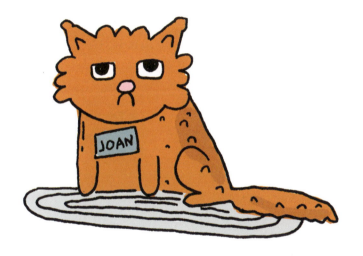

ARE YOU A TERRIBLE FRIEND?

This checklist will help you determine if you have earned the Worst Friend Award.

☐ YOU ARE ALWAYS LATE.

☐ YOU NEVER BRING A DISH TO POTLUCKS BUT YOU DO EAT EVERYTHING.

☐ YOU POINT OUT HOW PROBLEMATIC LADIES' NIGHTS ARE WHILE AT THE LADIES' NIGHT.

☐ YOU NEVER RESPOND TO GROUP TEXTS.

☐ YOU TALK SHIT ABOUT YOUR FRIENDS WHEN THEY AREN'T AROUND.

☐ YOU ONCE TOLD YOUR BEST FRIEND HER BABY LOOKS WEIRD.

☐ YOU TREAT YOUR FRIENDS' KITCHENS LIKE OPEN BARS.

☐ YOU NEVER OFFER TO DRIVE. ANYWHERE.

☐ YOU BORROW YOUR FRIENDS' COATS AND RETURN THEM COVERED IN CAT HAIR.

☐ YOU AREN'T INQUISITIVE ABOUT YOUR FRIENDS' LIVES. YOU ARE, HOWEVER, VERY INQUISITIVE ABOUT THEIR PETS' LIVES.

Did you check seven or more boxes? Congrats! You've earned the Worst Friend Award. You get to stay home with your cat tonight because your friends can't handle your shit anyway.

STEP 3

GET AN F AT YOUR JOB

If you're anything like me, you work to live, not the other way around. You survive paycheck to paycheck, and you fantasize daily about telling your boss, "I quit! Also, I never filled the coffeepot when it got low, and I stole a lot of toilet paper from the supply closet."

And coworkers are the worst. I mean, I sort of like that guy who always gives me the potato chips his wife packs him for lunch, but everyone else is terrible. Some of them actually try to be good at their jobs. Ugh. That's gross. I guess the old saying is true: "Keep your friends close and your enemies closer and your coworkers really, really far away."

We shouldn't have to work. Life's too short! But if you do have to trudge to an office every day, this chapter will teach you how to put in the absolute least amount of effort.

You're the worst-performing employee.
I've never been more proud of myself.

Bad Employee Tip #1

Pie charts aren't as delicious as they sound, but they are a good way to communicate your job dissatisfaction to your boring coworkers.

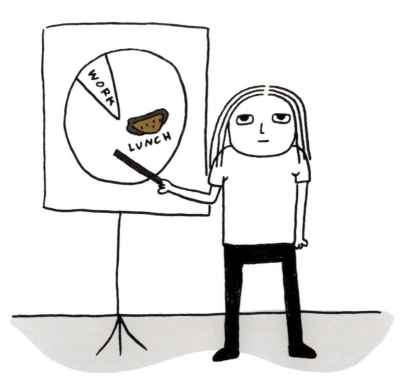

But why can't I have a
lunch day with a __work__ hour?

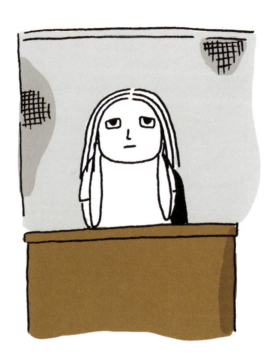

9 AM: Arrive at work
9:01 AM—4:59 PM: Existential crisis
5 PM: Leave work

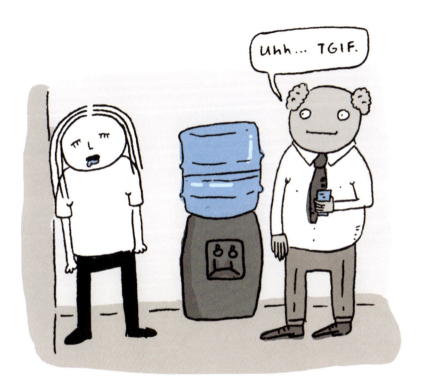

All week I can't wait to go out on Friday night, until Friday night, when I just want to sleep.

PLACES TO EAT YOUR LUNCH ALONE IN PEACE

1 Car

2 Bathroom

3 Janitor's closet

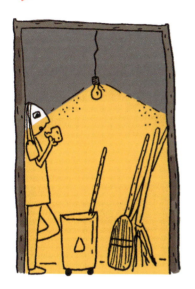

4 Office roof

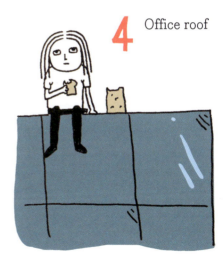

MOT
IV
ATION

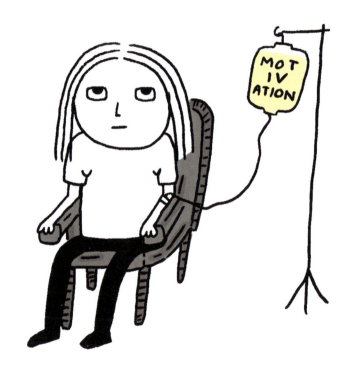

My Monday thru Friday.

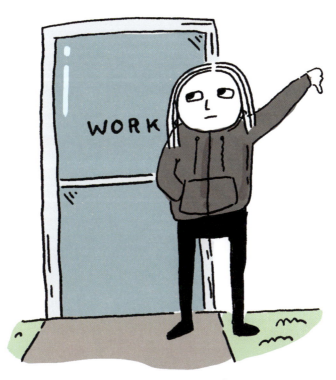

Screw this place. I'm _NEVER_ _EVER_ coming back! You hear me? See you in the morning.

Bad Employee Tip #2

Do not engage with your coworkers.
Your cubicle plant is the only friend
you need.

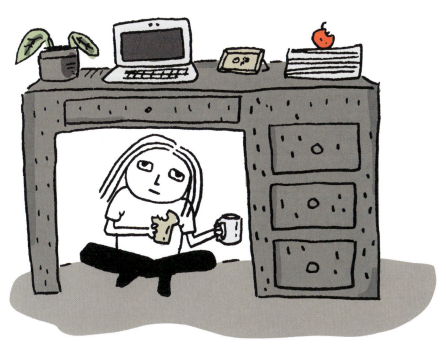

This is the part of my day when I
reflect on all the mistakes I made
in my early twenties that led me here.

EXCUSES TO USE WHEN CALLING IN "SICK" TO WORK

1 I'm sick (of showing up).

2 I'm sweating a lot. Like, a *lot*.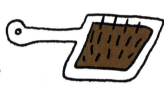

3 Bad hair day. That's valid, right?

4 Def caught something from Janet.

5 Free lunch gave me food poisoning. It's all your fault.

6 I'm dehydrated.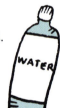

7 An eyelash is permanently stuck in my eye.

8 I ran out of toilet paper, so I'm stuck on the toilet.

9 My cat ran away. (To the next room. She likes her space.)

10 I watched a documentary about outer space and thought, "What's the point?"

11 Carsick.

12 Seasick.

13 Planesick.

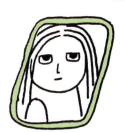

14 Trainsick.

15 Segwaysick.

16 Ubersick.

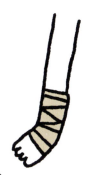

17 I sprained my ankle. For real this time.

18 I have nothing to wear. Seriously. I haven't done laundry in months.

19 I'm busy preparing for the weekend.

20 I've got the Whoopi cough.*

*COUGH THAT SOUNDS LIKE WHOOPI GOLDBERG'S LAUGH

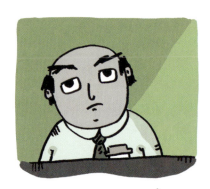

YOU'RE LATE!

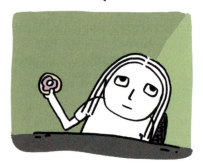

I'M ALWAYS LATE.
THIS IS JUST THE DAY I
GOT CAUGHT.

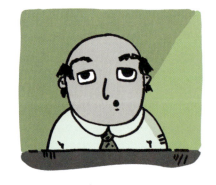

OH...

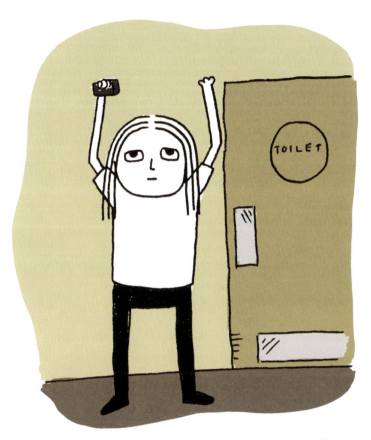

Just spent twenty minutes looking at Instagram in the bathroom!

Bad Employee
Tip #3

Look for another job while at your current job. That way, it's like you're getting paid to plan your escape.

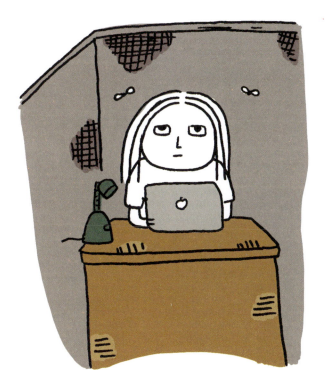

It's a beautiful day to rot
in my cubicle.

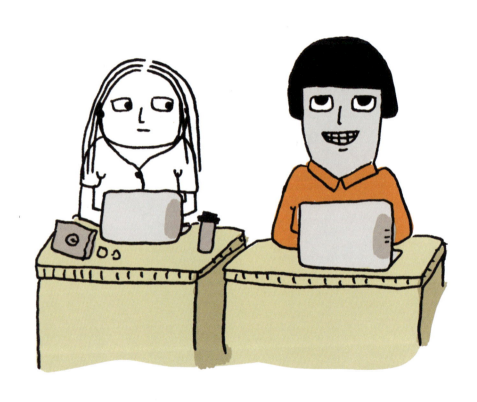

My happy coworkers scare me.

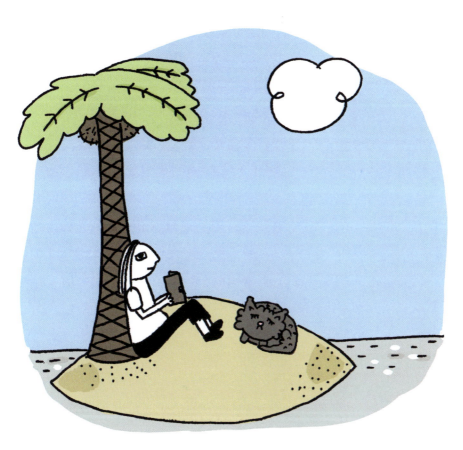

Out of office e-mail: Bye forever.

ARE YOU THE WORST EMPLOYEE?

- -

This checklist will help you determine if you have succeeded at failing at work.

☐ YOU SHOWED UP LATE FOUR OUT OF FIVE DAYS LAST WEEK.

☐ YOU REGULARLY PARK IN YOUR BOSS'S SPOT.

☐ YOU MAKE A HABIT OF REMINDING EVERYONE YOU'RE TOO GOOD FOR THIS JOB.

☐ YOU STEAL OFFICE SUPPLIES AND SELL THEM ON THE BLACK MARKET.

- [ ] YOU ONLY SAY "HAPPY BIRTHDAY" IF THERE'S FREE CAKE INVOLVED.

- [ ] YOU BRING YOUR CAT TO WORK EVEN THOUGH YOUR COWORKERS ARE ALLERGIC.

- [ ] YOU IGNORE LABELS ON FOOD IN THE REFRIGERATOR AND EAT WHATEVER YOU WANT.

- [ ] YOU SPEND APPROXIMATELY THREE-QUARTERS OF THE DAY JUDGING YOUR COWORKERS.

- [ ] YOU SPEND THE REMAINING QUARTER ON SOCIAL MEDIA.

- [ ] YOU NEVER REFILL THE COFFEE MACHINE.

Did you check seven or more boxes? Congrats! You've officially earned an F at work. Maybe you're even the Worst Employee of the Month! Wasn't that fun?

STEP 4

WRECK YOUR HEALTH

According to a new study I just made up, we think about working out and eating right 800 percent more than we actually do it. I'm sure there's some list of inspirational quotes backed by a bunch of Division I football coaches to encourage you to exercise and eat kale, but I'd like to offer an alternative: Throw in the sweaty towel. I mean, why not? Like I said, it's sweaty. No need to carry that around. It's just gross.

And besides, you can drink your green drinks and go to your dark, EDM-bumping spin class every day of your life, but all of our books end the same way. With an epilogue. Just kidding! With dying alone, obviously.

So sit back, absolutely don't get up, pop open a bag of potato chips, and read this chapter about doing exactly that. You'll learn almost nothing. It's brilliant.

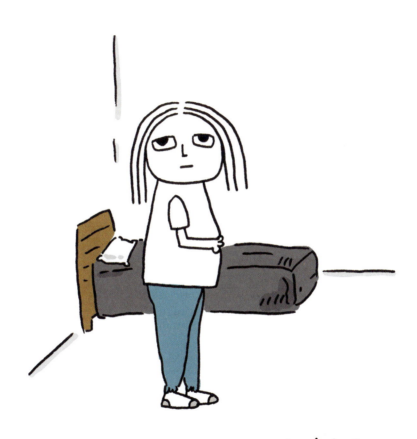

Almost back to my pre-food baby weight.

Glutton Tip #1

BYOSnacks when you go to your lactose-intolerant, vegan friend's birthday party.

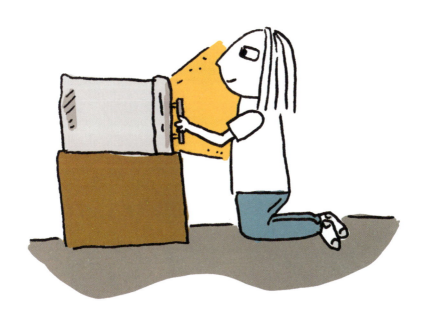

Not into Hot Yoga.
More into Hot Pockets.

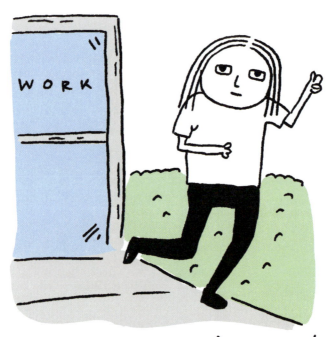

The only workout I'm doing today is when I yell "Work...out" when I leave the office.

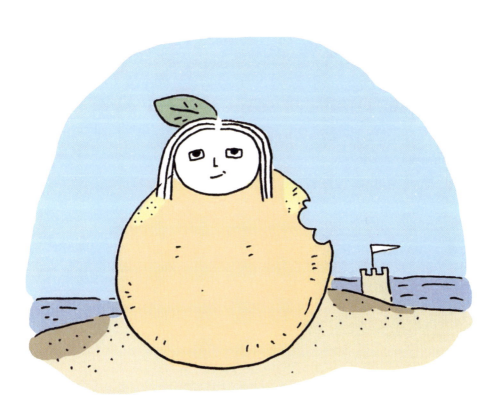

I'm gonna forgo a Beach Body
for a Peach Body. Round & fuzzy.

WHAT I SHOULD'VE BOUGHT INSTEAD OF MY UNUSED GYM MEMBERSHIP

1 48 pairs of sweatpants

2 A no-technology retreat for my cat

3 Massage chair installed into car

4 More TV streaming subscriptions

5 Video games (pressing buttons on a controller is totally a workout)

6 A 1995 Buick

7 A house in Normal, Illinois

8 A treadmill (to use as a rack for my 48 pairs of sweatpants)

9 A cheeseburger

10 So much Bitcoin

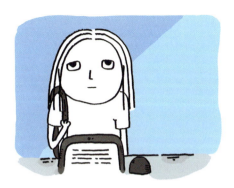

HERE'S THE DEAL:
YOU TAKE MONEY FROM ME EVERY MONTH
AND YOU NEVER SEE ME AGAIN.

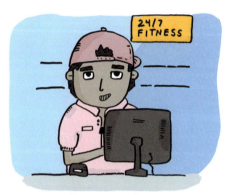

YOU GOT IT!

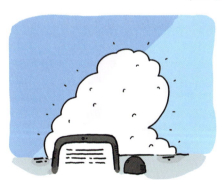

(CLOUD OF SMOKE APPEARS)

Glutton Tip #2

Put a "Start" sign on your couch
and a "Finish" sign on your fridge.
Look, you just won a race!

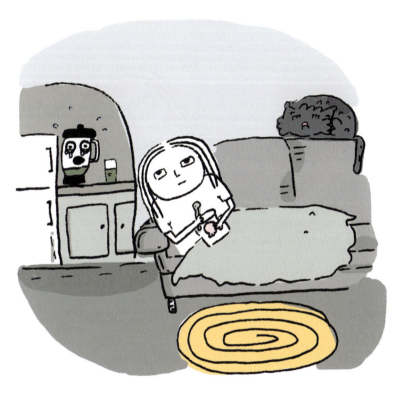

I have a terrible relationship with diets.
I always cheat on them.

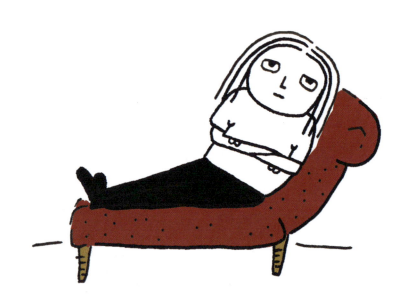

I consider this <u>physical</u> therapy
because I have to physically leave
my bed to get here.

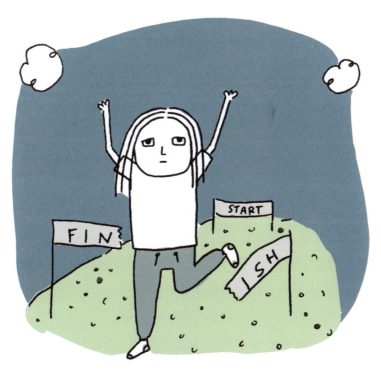

I like my workouts like I
like my eggs...
Over & Easy.

Glutton Tip #3

Get a delivery person who
does bed deliveries.

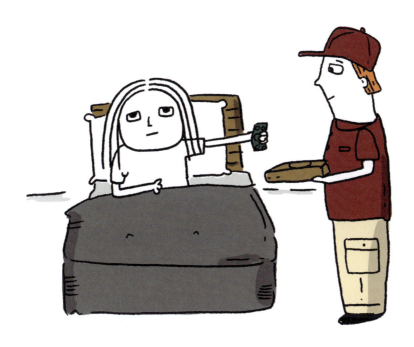

Treat yourself like a Garbage Queen on the weekends.

SINGLE-PERSON DINNERS THAT WILL IMPRESS NOBODY

1 Microwavable spaghetti

2 Half of that sandwich from earlier

3 Chips, salsa, and cheese cubes

4 Buffet of Pop-Tarts AKA Buffet of Despair

5 Boxed wine

6 Cereal crumbs with milk dregs

7 Stale bread with three drops of tears for sodium

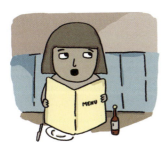

NO PICKLES.

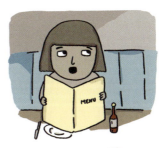

NO DRESSING.

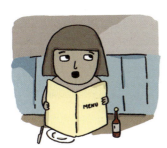

NO TOMATOES.

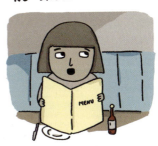

NO BREAD.

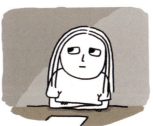

I'LL TAKE ALL OF HER REJECTIONS.

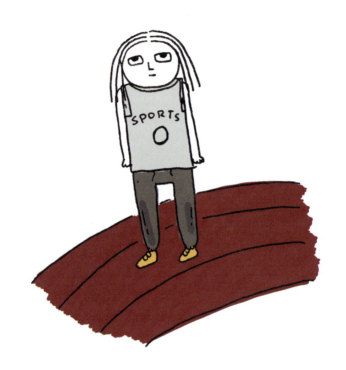

For the 10th year in a row,
"Run a Marathon" tops my list
of New Year's resolutions.
NOTE: Haven't run a mile since 7th grade.

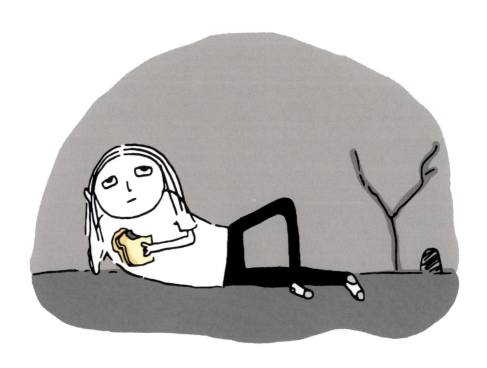

You don't need to work out if you
put a blanket in a duvet cover today.

HAVE YOU COMPLETED YOUR TRANSFORMATION INTO A COUCH POTATO?

This checklist will help you determine if you have mastered the art of vegetating.

☐ YOU WALKED INTO YOUR GYM IN SWEATPANTS AND DEMANDED TO CANCEL YOUR MEMBERSHIP.

☐ YOU ORDER PIZZA FOR DELIVERY WHILE YOU'RE STILL ON YOUR WAY HOME (THIS ONE'S FOR THE ADRENALINE JUNKIES).

☐ YOU BURNED YOUR SWIMSUITS IN A PUBLIC PLACE.

☐ YOU WALK WHEN YOU'RE SUPPOSED TO RUN.

☐ YOU SIT WHEN YOU'RE SUPPOSED TO WALK.

☐ YOU LIE DOWN WHEN YOU'RE SUPPOSED TO SIT.

☐ YOU BUY THE CEREAL YOU ALWAYS WANTED AS A KID. THE KIND THAT'S BASICALLY COOKIES.

☐ YOU'VE TRAINED YOUR CAT TO FETCH YOU FOOD.

☐ YOU ASPIRE TO SET A WORLD RECORD FOR "NOT WORKING OUT."

☐ YOU SIGN UP FOR 5K RACES JUST FOR THE FREE T-SHIRTS.

Did you check seven or more boxes? Congrats! You've officially thrown in the sweaty towel.

AVOID ROMANCE LIKE THE PLAGUE

Online dating was supposed to make things easier, but somehow romance is harder than ever. All you have to do is swipe, hook up, and repeat, but with that comes a whole new bag of problems—the inevitable "Sup, girl?" openings, unsolicited nudes, deceptive photos, and every lie in the book.

Besides, people get boring when they fall in love. They become horribly optimistic and never stop smiling. Do you want that for your life? No! It's much more fun to be the single friend forever and enjoy a lifetime of no-share pizza and ample bed space.

If you're in a relationship or are even thinking about getting into one, it's time to stop, drop, and roll out. In this chapter I'll show you how to set your romantic life on fire and watch it gloriously explode.

YEP, STILL SINGLE

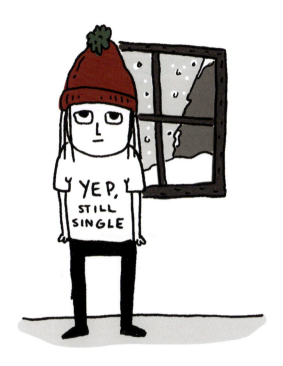

(Family Holiday Outfit)

Love Cynic Tip #1

Show photos of your pet to your
date. If they seem weirded out,
throw your drink in their face.

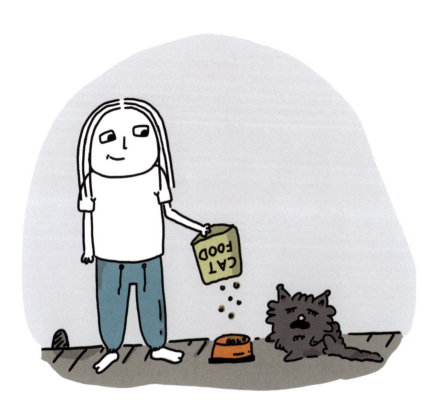

I only respond to one kind of cat call.

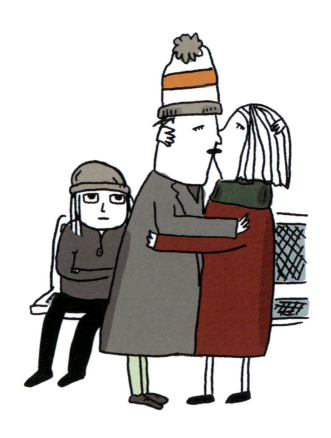

If you're happy and you know it,
keep that shit to yourself.

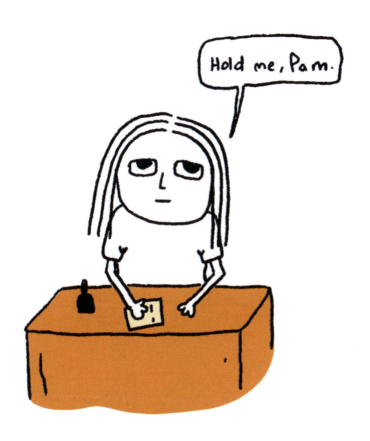

I only get manicures to experience the feeling of holding hands.

THINGS YOU SHOULD DEFINITELY SAY ON A FIRST DATE IF YOU WANT TO AVOID A SECOND DATE

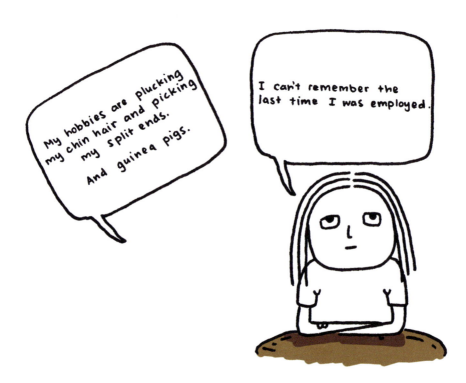

I forgot my wallet. Can I mail you a check?
On a typical Friday night I'm itching a rash. You?
What kind of music do I listen to? Exclusively early Creed.
I LOVE GUINEA PIGS!

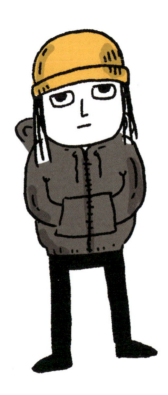

You know you're single when
your mom is your emergency contact.

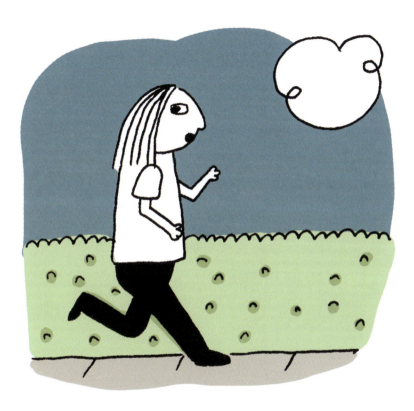

Directly after a date tells me
they don't like cats,

Love Cynic Tip #2

Watch rom-coms ironically. Loudly say things like "Ha! Nobody's that genuine!" and "Give that marriage three years. He's clearly in love with his best friend."

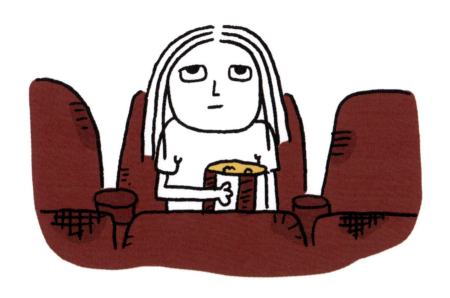

First comes love,
then comes marriage,
then comes baby,
I'm so alone.

HOW TO BREAK UP

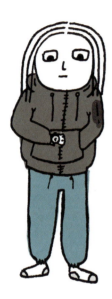

1 Decide it's time to bounce.

2 Watch movies about breaking up to prepare yourself. Memorize lines like "Frankly, my dear, I don't give a damn."

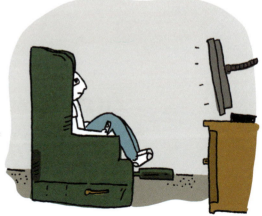

3 Get groceries. You'll need them later.

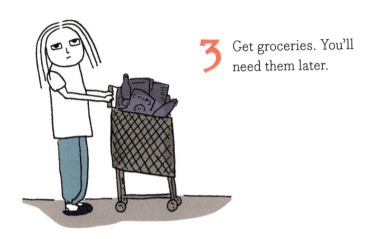

4 Text your boo and tell them you're out.

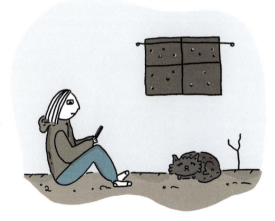

5 Wait till they go to work, and then creep around their house and say goodbye to their pets.

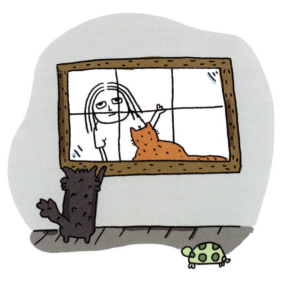

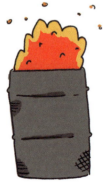

6 Burn your phone.

7 Eat those groceries.

Love Cynic Tip #3

Don't date online.

Or offline.

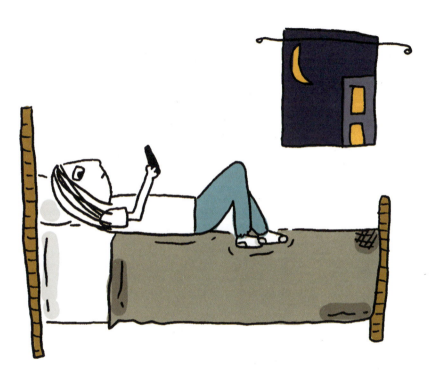

Just sent my first sext.
It was a photo of a cheese Danish.

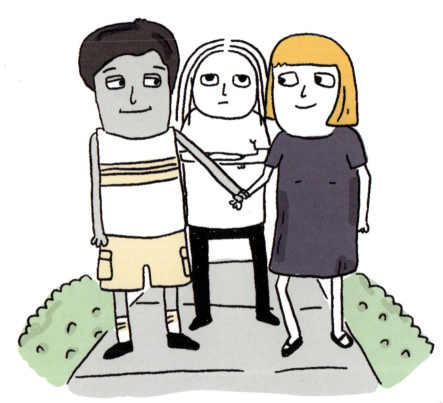

Holding hands while walking should be illegal.

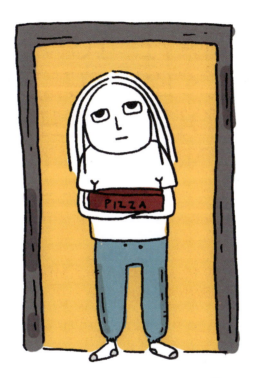

Domino's pizza app > Tinder
because I can see the progress.

HAVE YOU SUCCESSFULLY AVOIDED THE ROMANCE PLAGUE?

- -

This checklist will help you determine if you have mastered the art of being single.

☐ YOU ARE ABLE TO STRETCH IN BED WITHOUT HITTING ANOTHER HUMAN.

☐ YOU WAKE UP TO MEOWS INSTEAD OF HELLOS.

☐ NOBODY IS SPENDING YOUR MONEY BUT YOU.

☐ YOUR OBJECT OF AFFECTION IS A BAG OF POTATO CHIPS.

- ☐ YOUR FRIENDS HAVE STOPPED GIVING YOU A "PLUS ONE" WHEN THEY INVITE YOU TO THEIR WEDDINGS.

- ☐ INSTEAD OF DRUNK TEXTING YOUR EX, YOU DRUNK EMAIL YOUR TAX ACCOUNTANT.

- ☐ YOU DON'T HAVE TO CHECK IN WITH ANYONE BEFORE MAKING A TERRIBLE DECISION.

- ☐ YOU HAVE SEVERAL HOUSEPLANTS.

- ☐ YOUR SHAMPOO LASTS FOREVER.

- ☐ YOU PREFER ONION RINGS TO WEDDING RINGS.

Did you check seven or more boxes? Congrats! You've officially avoided the plague. Your prize? Watching whatever you want on Netflix, uninterrupted.

HOW TO GET LAUGHS FROM THE GRAVE

Okay, so we're all gonna die and that totally sucks. But death doesn't have to be scary. Like life, it can be mildly amusing. Like a pun or a dad joke. So why not go out with a laugh? With the right grave, you can make the cemetery your comedy stage.

Here are some tombstones that will entertain visitors, passing strangers, and graveyard ghosts.

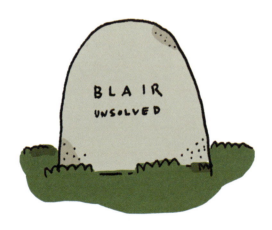

I WANT PEPPERONI
ON MY TOMBSTONE.

SHE DIED
DOING WHAT
SHE LOVED.

SLEEPING.

THAT JUICE CLEANSE
DIDN'T DO SHIT.

Jukebox Tombstone

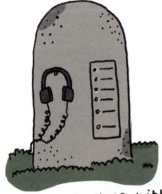

Feel your feelings with some sad music.

TV Tombstone

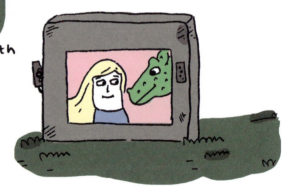

Catch up on your favorite shows while visiting your favorite ghost.

Vending Machine Tombstone

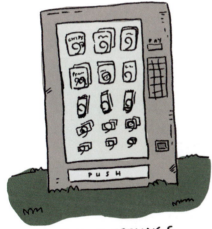

EAT YOUR FEELINGS.

Sports Tombstone

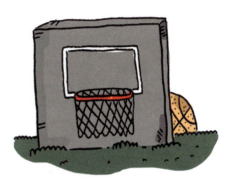

A good way to rebound from some sorrow.

131

Are you more of an urn person? Don't worry. I've got you covered, too. If there are any loved ones you didn't manage to shake off during life, prank them with this cute cookie jar urn.

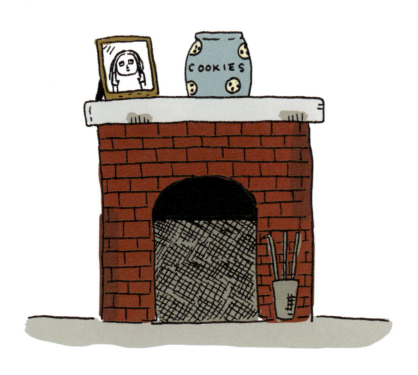

C'mon, you've urned this laugh.

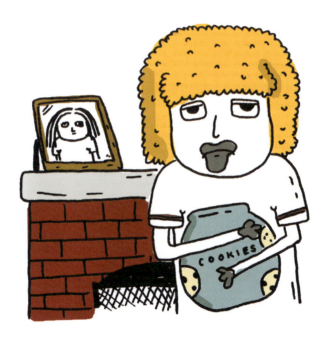

ACKNOWLEDGMENTS

Thanks to the original fans of Blair. Your beautiful messages and words of encouragement have changed the course of my career and filled the gaping hole in my heart.

To all my exes who dumped me—that tornado of heartbreak led to me drawing Blair.

To Workman Publishing—Evan Griffith is the perfect cat-loving editor. Thank you for fixing my grammatical errors because I really don't like commas and I also love a run-on sentence shout out to public school anyways thank you so much Evan you're magniffisent (sp?).

To Anthony Mattero for getting this going and believing in it. Your positivity would really turn Blair off.

To Justin Letter for working very hard to convince me to be confident in my work. Fat chance!

To my smart and amazing grandparents Ed and Mary Mangan.

Lastly, to my mom, Mary—as a single mother of five, it was hard to keep track of us, but you always managed to find and pick up the little comics I drew. And throw them away. All that garbage led to this book.

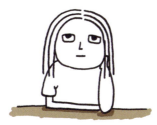

Ugh. Is this section over yet? I'm hungry and all this love is making me lose my appetite.